About the Author

I am a thirty-four-year-old junior doctor working in London. I have a background in Psychology and have always been fascinated by the physical and mental workings of the human body. It is from this standpoint that I deliver a personal account of my own health journey through a challenging and often stigmatised condition which has both physical and mental consequences on those affected.

Dr Siobhan O'Sullivan

My Life on Pause

Olympia Publishers
London

www.olympiapublishers.com
OLYMPIA PAPERBACK EDITION

Copyright © Dr Siobhan O'Sullivan 2023

The right of Dr Siobhan O'Sullivan to be identified as author of this work has been asserted in accordance with sections 77 and 78 of the Copyright, Designs and Patents Act 1988.

All Rights Reserved

No reproduction, copy or transmission of this publication
may be made without written permission.
No paragraph of this publication may be reproduced,
copied or transmitted save with the written permission of the publisher,
or in accordance with the provisions
of the Copyright Act 1956 (as amended).

Any person who commits any unauthorised act in relation to
this publication may be liable to criminal
prosecution and civil claims for damage.

A CIP catalogue record for this title is
available from the British Library.

ISBN: 978-1-80439-106-8

The information in this book has been compiled by way of general guidance only. Neither the author nor the publisher shall be liable or responsible for any loss or damage allegedly arising from any information or suggestion in this book.

First Published in 2023

Olympia Publishers
Tallis House
2 Tallis Street
London
EC4Y 0AB

Printed in Great Britain

My Life on Pause

Dedication

I dedicate this book to all of the strong women in my life. In loving memory of Grandma (May 1933-February 2022).

Acknowledgements

Thank you to my mum for encouraging me to write this book and get my message heard. Thank you to both my mum and dad for your ongoing support in all that I do.

For all of the strong women in my life.

In loving memory of Grandma
(May 1933-February 2022)

You taught me to be strong when the world could look so bleak,
You showed me how to move on when inside I felt so weak,
In you I saw compassion towards all those you held dear,
Whatever life would throw you would never show any fear,
As a child I was cared for in every single way,
And this love grew into a friendship I will cherish every day,
You always had time to listen and then you'd have your say,
Your honesty and wisdom helped guide me along the way,
You were always understanding to everyone in your life,
You held us all together as grandma, mother and wife,
You are adored in this world and the world above,
And now we must find comfort that your back with your true love,
Right now, it seems impossible to get up and carry on,
But through the lessons that you taught us, your spirit will live on.

Foreword

I believe in empowering women to have a voice. In a world where we face so many daily challenges, I believe the best way to overcome these is together, supporting one another every step of the way. I am thirty-four, and at the age of thirty-one, I was diagnosed with primary ovarian failure, which led to an early menopause. I am still on a journey trying to figure this all out. It can be a lonely road, and it is not a conversation that is often had. I want to change this so anyone going through the same thing feels they have some support and they have somewhere to turn. In a world where we are constantly being pushed to move forward, it is easy to sometimes get left behind. Just remember you are not alone.

Menopause

The menopause is your last menstrual period. Many people think of the menopause as the time leading up to or after their last period.

It is a process that can take many years, the periods become less frequent until they eventually stop. You are said to have gone through the menopause when you have been free of periods for one year.

Early Menopause

Most women in the UK go through the menopause at the age of fifty-one, you are considered to have gone through an early menopause if it happens before the age of forty-five.

Some causes for an early menopause include a hysterectomy (if you have surgery to remove your womb), oophorectomy (if you have surgery to remove your ovaries), cancer treatments (chemotherapy or radiotherapy), hereditary links and in some no cause is found.

Primary Ovarian Insufficiency

Primary ovarian insufficiency (POI) is when your ovaries stop producing normal amounts of oestrogen and thus stop working properly under the age of forty years. As a result, you may experience a premature menopause.

How common is POI?

POI affects approximately
 1 in 100 women under the age of forty
 1 in 1000 women under the age of thirty
 1 in 10,000 women under the age of twenty
 A natural spontaneous early menopause affects approximately 5% of the population before the age of forty-five.
 (Figures taken from hwww.daisynetwork.org)

Flirty Thirty and Flushes!

I'm enjoying my early thirties. I know many people fear the big 3-0, however, after years of trying to desperately "find myself" during my twenties, there is a certain satisfaction with hitting an age where you can finally own who you are. I had recently come out of a long-term relationship, and I was looking forward to a new decade, where I could unapologetically be myself and do things for me. Amidst the chaos of heartbreak, I had allowed my prescription of the contraceptive pill to lapse, and I found myself hormone free for the first time in over a decade. I remember the first flush like it was yesterday. I was sat on a busy train on a freezing cold morning in January, commuting to work with my coffee in hand. All of a sudden, a tsumami of heat flooded my body and I was desperately stripping off my coat and scarf in the middle of the carriage. I assumed it was due to the hot coffee, but five minutes later, when there was still sweat trickling down my brow and I was sat in nothing but a vest top, I figured something wasn't quite right. I was a newly qualified doctor at the time, and with my limited fertility knowledge, I assumed maybe coming off the pill had triggered my hormones to go into overdrive. It was only when the same kerfuffle began to happen on a daily basis that I thought it was maybe time to get some blood tests. I remember the initial call when a young male doctor, who quite evidently has as much knowledge on fertility as myself, informed me that there were some abnormalities with my blood tests and he would book me for some repeats. This was quite standard practise and I booked myself for another test. It was only months later when I had gone into the GP for my smear test that things started to spiral. I was sat with a senior female GP whilst she accessed my record, and I could see her facial expression change dramatically. With a look of almost pitied empathy she asked if I was aware that some of my blood results had been abnormal. I replied that I was. She then went on to tell me that she had never seen results quite like these in a women of my age. My FSH (follicle stimulating hormone) was in the high twenties, which she went on to explain was above what she'd expect to see for someone starting to go through the menopause. This was the first time someone had directly said the word "menopause". Here I was thinking I had come to the doctors for a simple smear, and now, this lady was throwing the prospect of menopause into the equation. She, then, quickly went on to say she was very concerned and was referring me to the "Primary Ovarian failure Clinic" for an urgent review.

Hearing the words "ovarian failure" really struck a nerve. "Early menopause" sounds so much softer, like you've eased into a natural phase of life a bit ahead of time, but "premature ovarian failure" hits you like a bus. There was this feeling of shock and almost terror. I had moved from a position of having a few abnormal blood results to confronting the very real possibility my ovaries were failing, and I'd had no idea it was happening. How as a woman does your body stop working and you are completely oblivious to it. All of a sudden, the freedom of my new-found thirties had turned very sour and I had no idea of what the future would hold.

Starting the conversation…

I am a thirty-four-year-old women who has been diagnosed with primary ovarian insufficiency (POI). I received this diagnosis when I was thirty-one, and I have been trying to understand and navigate it ever since. I have struggled over the years without even realising I am sometimes struggling and there haven't been many places where you can turn to for support. I am very lucky as I am surrounded by the most amazing family and friends who have been so supportive from the outset, but there's still part of me that is struggling to make sense of things. I think this comes from a lack of awareness that this issue exists. When you search the internet for "early menopause", you find blogs and articles about women going through the menopause in their forties. The menopause is a difficult time for any one at any age, but I don't think the awareness is there that this can happen to very young women long before they reach forty, and this conversation is a very different one to be had. Imagine knowing you can't give birth to a child before you've even started trying, before you've even met the person you might decide to have that child with. It can be a very lonely and a very isolating journey, and I think it affects more women that we know. On top of this, there is the issue of stigma. People not wanting other people to know this is an issue that is affecting them. I respect however anybody chooses to tackle these issues, be that openly or privately. It is your body and your story. However, I think that I find solace in talking things through and approaching things with an open heart. I hope that this book can help others as I try to open up conversations and navigate some of the complex emotions that this diagnosis brings into your life at such a young age.

Some Science: Hormones and the menopause

Women have hormones in their body that regulate their menstrual cycle and stimulate the production of eggs.

FSH is a hormone released by the pituitary gland which causes the maturation of eggs in the ovaries, and also, they release oestrogen from the ovaries.

Oestrogen stops Follicle Stimulating Hormone (FSH) production to allow for the development of one mature egg per cycle and stimulates the release of Luteinizing Hormone (LH).

LH causes the release of the mature egg from the ovary.

Progesterone maintains the lining of the uterus mid-cycle and throughout pregnancy should an egg implant.

In peri-menopause (the time leading up to menopause) hormones are all over the place. However, after the menopause, there is a dramatic fall in oestrogen levels and progesterone is no longer produced following the last menstrual period.

When diagnosing the menopause, an elevated FSH can be used to confirm this. If a women's FSH level is consistently raised above 30 mIU/ml and she has not had a menstrual period for a year, she is thought to have gone through the menopause.

There're no eggs left

I have to admit as soon as the words "ovarian failure" were thrown into the mix, the fear became very real. I have never been one of those women who is desperate to have children early on, and it's not even something I was even 100% sure I did definitely want, but as soon as someone tells you, you can't have something, your mindset automatically changes, and I knew I needed go get some answers and act fast. Sadly, for me, the waiting list was a long one and I couldn't get an appointment with a fertility specialist in the NHS for another six to eight months. This in my mind was a time precious issue, what happens if each day I was getting closer to the menopause and ultimate infertility. What happened if each day more and more eggs were withering away. I knew I had to get seen quickly so I could at least get my options on the table and get ahead. My body had already blindsided me and started this descent into menopause, I had to regain some control. I probably still had time to freeze some eggs, and then I wouldn't need to worry about this again until I was ready to unfreeze them and start a family when I was good and ready.

I managed to arrange an appointment online within a week with a fertility specialist in central London. I went on my own. Friends and family had offered to accompany me, but ultimately, this was something I felt I needed to face on my own. I was single and this was something I was going through by myself in my own body. I knew that I would get answers from the specialist and I was aware that some of these may not be the ones I wanted, but I almost couldn't face doing that with anyone else in the room. I needed to process whatever was said myself, and I couldn't worry about or manage anyone else's reactions alongside my own.

As a doctor I have had many "difficult conversations" with patients over the years. I've learnt the structure you are supposed to follow to break the "bad news", I've sat there and empathised with patients over things I can't even begin to imagine they are going through. Regardless of how much you prepare yourself for "the worst" in whatever situation you may find yourself in, I think it still stings when someone confirms your ultimate fear. I think part of me had hoped that even though my ovaries were "failing", we still had time to preserve some form of fertility, and then, life could get back on track. This had been a small hiatus, we could form a new plan and life could continue.

I told my story to the specialist, but within minutes, it was clear things were not going to just bounce back. We went over my blood results and symptoms again and I was advised it was highly likely I had "gone through" an early menopause. This was the first shock. I'd assumed it was a process that I was in the middle of transitioning through. I didn't realise I'd crossed the finish line without even realising I was part of the race. The specialist was direct but kind, they didn't give me false hope and they gave me practical options and steps to take. The compassion they showed I will remember forever and it made a very difficult conversation that little bit easier.

The next step was to get one more blood test to see if I had any eggs left and whether it would be possible to freeze them. I wasn't feeling hopeful, it was clear that things were more serious than I had initially anticipated, but this was one last speck of hope. I think when life seems dim, we all like to cling on to whatever light we can, even if deep down you know it's already starting to fade. The results were back within days, and the phone call came to follow "I'm really sorry but unfortunately the tests have shown you have no eggs left."

My Therapist Ghosted Me

I had been seeing a therapist for a few months before the menopause saga began to unfold. This was mainly spurred on by some naive dream that I could off load all of my emotional baggage onto a complete stranger who would then go on to solve each and every one of my various life dilemmas based on the premise they could understand me so well. The most I actually got out of these sessions was one good book recommendation. I was starting to have doubts that me and my therapist were maybe not the best fit and she wasn't fulfilling the idealistic dream I was chasing, but it wasn't until I decided to share my menopause story that the relationship ground to a halt.

As always at the start of the session she asked me how I had been and what was new in my life. At this point I decided to tell her about the blood tests and my recent diagnosis of an early menopause. She froze up, became slightly awkward and then fiddled with the air conditioning unit for ten minutes before giving out some valuable life advise about the importance of exercise and eating healthily to maintain good mental health. At this point our time was up, and she said she would be in touch to arrange my next appointment. Fast forward one month and several unanswered text messages later, and I came to terms with the fact our relationship was over.

My fertility specialist offered to refer me to a fertility therapist through the NHS but, once again, the waiting list was incredibly long. The first available appointment was a year after my original diagnosis.

I have since had a few phone sessions with this therapist (thanks to COVID, there have been no face to face appointments available) and she does keep checking in with me for which I am very grateful. It is finally nice to have someone who understands the process and will confront it with you rather than turn away. However, unfortunately, the reality remains that when I ultimately needed someone to speak to professionally in the initial stages of my diagnosis, the support wasn't there. By the time I had my first consultation with the NHS fertility therapist, I had already spent a year trying to deal with things myself, I'd had to as there was no other option. I was in a completely different head space; I was being asked the questions I wish I'd been asked at the time of diagnosis, but now a year on, I'd moved myself on. I'm not sure moving on alone was the healthiest option and I think some guidance early on would have helped me to confront the issues head on more at the time. Nevertheless, we are where we are and there's no point looking back with regrets.

It isn't anyone's fault. I don't blame the therapist who ghosted me for doing so. She must have felt out of her comfort zone, and wasn't sure how to help. This can be scary and I get that. The therapist I eventually talked too through the NHS offers some sound advice which I try to take on moving forward, sadly this just didn't initially align with my own personal journey and my own early need for support.

I'm still not sure what the best form of support is. It's not a subject talked about very much, and those that do talk about it are still usually a lot older than I am, and as a result have different fears and obstacles to overcome.

Searching for a reason

Once the shock of the diagnosis has hit, other concerns start to ease their way into your already overloaded mind. Why has this happened to me?

Is there something wrong that has caused this? With my limited medical fertility knowledge, I was starting to spiral. Could this be cancer? I wasn't even sure there was a cancer that could do this, but could there be? Could I have an undiagnosed genetic condition? What would this mean if I did? Did I have some sort of autoimmune condition that was attacking my insides without me knowing. Suddenly the problem didn't just seem to be about my ovaries and their failure. I couldn't believe I'd got so bogged down with this, what happens if this was just the surface of the problem, what happens if the real issue was much more severe and this was simply a symptom of a much more serious and potentially devastating disease. I had no idea why this was happening, and it was all so new to me, I didn't know this was something that could happen to someone of my age (despite my somewhat limited medical training on fertility). A lack of sufficient knowledge then allows your mind to run away with you, it starts catastrophizing the situation because in your head you can't quite make sense of any of it.

The specialist I went to see ran a whole host of blood tests, looking at my genetics, my immune function, my hormonal levels. He comprehensively covered every base he possibly could.

When I saw him back in clinic, he informed me all of those tests had come back clear. There had been no indication in any of my lab results to suggest why this had happened. He simply said that in some women we never find out a cause. The trigger is unknown. It could be down to the environment, to pollution, it could be down to a lifestyle choice, maybe a stressful life event. Sadly, there was no way of knowing.

There was a strange sense of relief.

But then, the self-doubt creeps in again. Had I done this to myself. Had I not looked after my body well enough, had I put something in there I shouldn't? Could stress have done this, I didn't consider myself a particularly "stressy" person, but every life has its stresses, had I not coped well enough with this? Had I been on the pill for too long, did I take the morning after pill one too many times? Should I not have moved to London with all the pollution, had living in cities for the last ten years poisoned my insides.

Writing this down now and reading it back, I can see how ridiculous this all sounds, but they were very real thoughts going through a very confused and desperate brain at that time.

What's more if I did have a new underlying condition what would the treatment for that be. I'd just got my head around the fact I would need to start HRT, what else would I need to take. If you are diagnosed with a chronic condition, it affects your whole life. Your lifestyle has to be amended to allow room for this condition. If you are diagnosed with diabetes, you have to find the time to monitor your blood sugars and manage this with insulin or medications. I think the impact of a regular lifelong medications are overlooked until you are faced with it yourself.

As it turned out I didn't need to manage any other underlying conditions. It just had to come to terms with the POI. Now I can see that regardless of the cause, there was nothing I could have done or could do to either predict or stop this from happening. You can't live your life in fear of what may happen, especially when you aren't aware of those potential risks and consequences. You can make good healthy life choices for your general overall health and well-being of course, but you can't predict all the possible outcomes of all your small life choices and you can't limit your life in doing so.

Some Science: Causes of POI

Genetic reasons- abnormalities with chromosomes or genes (e.g., Turners syndrome, Fragile X syndrome).

Endocrine conditions- hypoparathyroidism and hypoadrenalism.

Infectious processes (less frequent).

Surgery- previous pelvic surgery can lead to POI.

Autoimmune- your body has adrenal or ovarian antibodies, where your body's own cells attack organs and tissues from within.

Cancer treatments- previous chemotherapy or radiotherapy.

Picking your poison

At a time when it seemed that many choices had been cruelly taken away, the decision of which Hormone Replacement Therapy (HRT) to start allowed me to take back some of that control. One specialist advised strongly that I should consider a hormone patch, as this would deliver the most effective dose of the hormones needed. I politely declined. There was no way as a woman in my early thirties I wanted to walk around with a patch, I felt like I may has well have worn a badge saying "something's wrong with me I can't have children". People would evidently see a patch. I felt like this was a complete breach of my privacy, and at a time when I hadn't yet processed what was going on, I couldn't imagine openly sharing this with the world through a patch plastered openly on my skin. I know that we live in the UK and the number of days a year spent in a bikini are limited, but I wasn't ready to let this go yet. It was my diagnosis, my body, and I wasn't prepared to put it out there in any physical sense.

My next option was a hormonal cream designed to be used like a moisturiser every day after showering. This, again, felt like a restriction on my freedom. What if I didn't want to shower at the same time each day, what if I wanted to shower twice in one day. What if I was running late and didn't have time to shower before work. I couldn't commit solidly to a daily face care regime how on earth did they expect me to commit to an extended daily shower routine.

Every option they gave me felt like a hinderance to my life. I was still very much in the denial phase, I wasn't ready to accept I had a condition that needed to be treated. Any treatment that posed some imposition on my life I would outwardly reject. I understand saying this now seems childish and immature, but you don't always know why you are behaving the way you are in difficult situations; you can only unpick it at a later date when you've had time to process and reflect.

We reluctantly settled on a daily hormonal pill. I figured that as I'd managed to take the contraceptive pill for the last decade how different would this be. Also, if any one were to see this pill on my bedside cabinet or in my bathroom, I could pretend it was something else. I realise now most of this was about some misguided self-preservation, but it was what I needed to do at the time to get through it. One downside to this hormonal pill was that it wouldn't protect me against unwanted pregnancy. Now I know this seemed like a ridiculous worry in the current post-menopausal climate, however, I was warned there was always a very slim chance that fertility could improve and I couldn't be faced with any other unexpected surprises. I also needed to replace the progesterone in my body, which meant I had to get the Mirena coil inserted. This alone was quite possibly the most painful experience of my life so far, and I hope it is something I never need to put my body through again! It was almost like the hormones were having their revenge, maybe a patch didn't seem such a terrible idea any more.

Some Science: Hormone Replacement therapy (HRT)

Hormone replacement therapy (HRT) replaces the natural female hormones that are lost during the menopause.

There are different hormone preparations that can be taken, most women take a combination of oestrogen and progesterone, although, women who no longer have a womb can just take progesterone.

There are different methods of taking HRT, these include skin patches, tablets, gels, vaginal creams and vaginal pessaries.

There are different treatment plans, some women take continuous HRT and some take it in cycles.

Some Science: The Mirena Coil-Intrauterine contraceptive System (IUS)

The Intrauterine contraceptive System (IUS) or "contraceptive coil" is a small, flexible, plastic device which sits inside the womb (uterus). There are two threads attached to it which pass out through the neck of the womb (cervix) and lie in your. These allow you to check it is still there. They also mean it can be removed easily. They do not hang outside the body. The IUS contains a slow-release progestogen hormone called levonorgestrel (LNG). (www.patient.info)

Long term effects of HRT: The myth vs. the reality

When I realised, I would need to be on HRT for over a decade, I was concerned. To my knowledge, HRT was something you should only use for a short period just to get you through the menopause, it wasn't a mediation to be taken long term, this wasn't supposed to be a chronic disease!

Was it OK for me to be on synthetic hormones for the next twenty years of my life, that didn't seem natural, surely it couldn't be OK!

The myth vs. the reality...

HRT causes breast cancer- There is not an increased risk of BC for women who start HRT before the age of fifty. The risk remains the same for these women as those who have not yet gone through menopause and have natural amounts of oestrogen circulating in their bodies.

HRT Causes blood clots- although oral HRT can increase this risk slightly, if you are healthy and active, then this risk is very, very low.

HRT causes weight gain- there is no evidence that this is the case.

HRT long term can be harmful- if you enter an early menopause, then the benefits that HRT can give to your bones and heart are important, and not taking it could be more harmful to your overall health.

Loosing something you never had

Struggling with the concept that you can't have a child when you don't currently want a child is a bit of a minefield. It's hard to be asked to empathise with yourself for something you aren't sure if you actually want. It's the whole process of mourning something you don't have and aren't even really sure you were striving for. On reflection it's no wonder my original therapist ran a mile, how are you supposed to guide someone through all of that?

I have always been open to the idea of children, but that was always a concept for far in my future. I have a good job which requires a lot of my time and I want to achieve certain things before I start thinking about starting any sort of family. There's also a lot of the world I want to see before I have children and many, many things I want to do. As I've said before, it's never been my main focus to get married, have kids and start that life as soon as possible. I know many people who do have that dream and I fully support that. I also know people who place more of an emphasis on having that family life, and would be crushed to have that option taken away. That's not to say I'm not crushed and sometimes I think that makes it all more confusing. How do you navigate having something taken away when you are still trying to figure out your own life and how you want everything to fit into it. There's a strange sort of guilt associated with feeling sad about losing something you might not have even wanted.

There's another sort of guilt that can creep in when trying to manage the burden of other people's reactions. When you tell them you can't have children, and they appear more devastated than you, it throws all sorts of doubts in the air. Am I some sort of heartless monster for not sharing this exact emotive response? Should I be more devastated by this. It's hard to identify if your current emotion is a reaction to the present stage you are at in life, i.e., currently not looking to bear child, or if its rooted more deeply, i.e. I'm not that maternal and may never actually have wanted to bear child.

I have found since the diagnosis that I do almost feel more detached from the concept of motherhood, but I'm not sure whether that is just how I feel or whether my mind is switching into a protective mode and shielding me from a wandering down a path that could potentially open up more hurt and pain.

Boxing things up!

After my first consultation with the specialist doctor, I was given a book to take away and read "Making Friends with the Menopause."

As soon as I got home, this book went into a box. The problem was I didn't want to make friends with the menopause. Why would I want to make friends with something that I hadn't invited into my life? I didn't need to read any books on something I could easily shut away and ignore.

    It took me over two years to take that book out of the box. I decided that I needed to try a bit harder to accept and understand what was going on in my body. I have spent the last few years pushing things down and trying to get on with life. I didn't want this diagnosis to define me or take over my life. However, by adopting this attitude, I also hadn't given myself time to accept or process what it was all about. I had tried to deal with the situation emotionally without taking any time to understand the physical implications. I decided to take the book out of the box and begin my journey into understanding what the menopause was all about.

Unexplained emotions at an unexpected time

There aren't many resources that you can turn to gain an insight into the menopause, there are even less looking at it from the perspective of someone under the age of forty. Nonetheless, the resources you do find often talk about emotional changes particularly in the perimenopausal period. Women talk about the uncertainty of their emotions and the stresses associated with this at a difficult time in their lives. Throughout all the resources I have read surrounding this issue, there is still a focus on early menopause affecting women aged forty to forty-five. The emotional challenges this group of women face are often completely different to the emotional challenges faced in your late twenties/early thirties. Regardless of age, all women going through perimenopause often report struggling with the ability to attach a specific reason to their emotions and all seem to have initial difficulty in making that connection between emotional lability and onset of the dreaded pause.

Now imagine obliviously going through all the emotional turmoil of the perimenopause before you even knew you could. Mood swings up and down, anxiety, low self-worth, uncontrollable anger, these are all some of the emotional symptoms that can be attributed to the fluctuating hormone levels in your body. The scary thing is that although these your poor innocent self you are a good fifteen years away from a menopausal hot flush. In the various literature there are tips and tricks for how to manage hot flushes, how to reduce them, how to avoid triggers, but at an age when you are struggling to connect the dots, how can you implement these lifestyle changes. You aren't even aware you should need to.

What's more, many of these suggested changes include avoiding caffeine (which is breakfast for most people in their thirties) and avoiding alcohol (which is not on the radar as you leave your wild twenties behind). Whilst these life changes you may be willing to accept later on in life as you approach the inevitable "change", as a young woman entering her thirties, these triggers form an integral part of your life and social circles. The thought of being forced to stop them seems even more unjust and unfair. I think when you go through anything at a time when it is unexpected you naturally kick back with the mentality "I didn't ask for this, I don't need to accept it or change my life because of it." The sad thing is that life doesn't work like that and the more you push back the worse things get. You have to come to terms with life changes and learn to make them work for you rather than pushing back against them. The day you finally let go to this resistance is the most liberating day of your life.

The other issue with experiencing a hot flush at the age of thirty is the sheer embarrassment. You are too young to go through this process and you don't want anyone to be aware. To compound the ultimate confusion you find yourself in, trying to figure out what is going on with your body, you then have to navigate how you communicate this with the world. A hot flush doesn't give you the time or space to work that out. It is the most obvious and uncontrollable situation you can find yourself in. You have to strip down wherever you are in time, whilst sweat pours from your brow, there's no way of being inconspicuous about that, and if anyone finds a way please do share. As a young woman it takes time yourself to process the fact you are entering an early menopause, what happens if you aren't yet ready to share with the whole world. However, it feels like your body isn't giving you that choice, it feels like it's almost working against you in that sense. It feels like a betrayal of the worst kind. You and your body are meant to be one, but your body is not considering your privacy and confidentiality or your autonomy to choose who you share this change with. It is leaving you as exposed as it possibly could and you're there on your own trying frantically to pick up the pieces as you redress and avoid eye contact with everyone sat on the train.

may be expected in women approaching fifty, in your twenties and thirties you would never think that the root cause of these emotions was linked to an unprecedented decline in your fertility.

I was thirty-one when I first got diagnosed with premature ovarian insufficiency (POI), and by the time the diagnosis came, it was assumed that I had already gone through the menopause. So when had the process begun? How had my body gone through this whole hormonal upheaval and I'd been totally oblivious until it was too late? Had I rode the wave of emotional instability really well and come out the other side unscathed. It's made me reflect back on my late twenties, the time I must have been going through the perimenopausal period. I was on the Combined Oral Contraceptive Pill (COCP) at the time, so had some of these hormonal changes been masked by the extra hormones I was consuming into my body. I have always been an emotional person and not scared to show my feelings rather than masquerade them, but I started to question had this been the real me or was this the emotional rollercoaster of menopause rearing its ugly head. I look back at various relationships I had with friends, partners and family members and wonder how much this unconscious "perimenopause" had a role to play. Sometimes I would have a short temper and sometimes my emotions were disproportionate to the situation at hand. No one would have ever thought that the hormonal changes associated with POI would affect a woman this young, how many women are currently going through this ignorant emotional hell unable to find the answer because no one is looking in the right place? Often when younger women demonstrate emotion they are tarred with the "time of the month" brush, which in itself is a chauvinistic outdated term of phrase. Imagine having to navigate this emotional dysregulation and combat these negative connotations on a daily basis at a time when society doesn't have an accepted explanation for your behaviour. No one expects you to be going through the menopause at thirty, so society doesn't allow for you too. Women are often judged for showing emotion and not "having a grip" on them. How many women are belittled and ostracised for unpredictable emotional behaviour when they aren't receiving the support and recognition they perhaps need and deserve.

Your twenties are already an emotional battleground, you may have started your professional life, you may be getting married, thinking about starting a family, you may be a student with the ongoing stresses of exams. I was studying for medicine in my late twenties, I look back now and wonder how much of my struggles at this time could have been related to the perimenopause. Symptoms such as brain fog, forgetfulness, anxiety and stress; it's hard to retrospectively go back and try and attach significance and meaning to symptoms and behaviours you that may or may not have been related. I think that I was relatively lucky, I managed to get through this period of my life without too much upheaval, but there must be women going through it now who may not be so lucky and have no idea why they are feeling the way they do. Without raising an awareness that menopause can happen at such a young age, we risk alienating those people who are going through it and, understandably, have no idea that they are.

Some Science: Hot flush

Hot flushes occur in about three in four women. A typical hot flush (or flash) lasts a few minutes and causes flushing of your face, neck and chest. You may also sweat (perspire) during a hot flush. Some women become giddy, weak, or feel sick during a hot flush. Some women also develop a 'thumping heart' sensation (palpitations) and feelings of anxiety during the episode. The number of hot flushes can vary from every now and then, to fifteen or more a day. Hot flushes tend to start just before the menopause and can persist for several years.

(www.patient.info)

The Infamous "Hot Flush"

If any one symptom could be attributed to the menopause, it would surely be the "hot flush". I can't tell you how many times I have seen women getting flushed in public and someone making the jibe "are you going through the menopause?" Even now in my early thirties if I have a hot flush at work or with friends who aren't aware, they will still joke "going through the menopause, are we?" and the sad thing is they are so naively unaware that this could be a real possibility and their words could actually trigger a hurtful response.

As I've mentioned before the first sign that I had something wasn't right was the horrendous hot flushes on the train on my way to work. It's not just a case of "overheating", your body feels like it's on fire, it's like nothing you've ever experienced before, which is why it often triggers women to get themselves checked over.

Hot flushes are an awful experience at any age, but it's fair to say that they are more anticipated as a woman approaches a certain stage of her life. The confusion you go through in your early thirties, when all of a sudden, your body is a live furnace, is monumental. There's an immediate sense of panic "what's wrong with me", because as a woman you usually know when something's not right. However, at this age you don't automatically make the connection between the menopause, why would you, to up telling yourself you probably are. You, again, enter into an unhealthy relationship with your own body where you feel it is acting against you and you aren't one in the same.

Forgetfulness is another hidden symptom. This is still something I contend with to this day, it's not terrible and not debilitating forgetfulness, but I do need to prompt myself sometimes or set reminders as I can predict the things I will inevitably forget! The good thing is that to tackle this you need to keep your mind and body active, which at a younger age are things that are maybe easier to achieve. So, although, I often talk about the disadvantages of going through the change at such a young age, there may be a few hidden silver linings along the way which you have to grasp when you can.

Possibly the most confusing, most embarrassing and misunderstood symptom I did have to contend was a loss of bladder control. I remember for a while in my twenties having stress incontinence and I couldn't for the life of me understand why. If I used a skipping rope during a training session, I would always have a little leak. It was mortifying. I remember specifically one day going to a trampoline park and hating the whole experience, because with every bounce I felt a little bit of fluid leak into my underwear. I felt so self-conscious and so dirty, we were asked if we wanted to extend our session and I had to make an excuse as to why I couldn't stay longer. All women are aware of stress incontinence, but it is usually something experienced post childbirth or as you approach a later stage of life. I couldn't understand why my pelvic floor was weak at such a young age, I did my pelvic floor exercises! I was so embarrassed to talk about this with anyone and I kept it all bottled in. This miscommunication with your body and misunderstanding of what your body is actually going though is so unhealthy. It again puts a barrier between you and your body. You resent it for putting you through these things, but that's because you don't understand what's happening to it.

Ultimately the danger of not having an awareness is that rather than working with your body to find solutions, you turn against her and that's not helpful to anyone. If women are more aware of some of the hidden symptoms of menopause, it may help them to better understand their bodies and their journeys and to have a healthier relationship with the whole process. This is true at any age but particularly at an age when the journey starts a little too soon.

Some Science: Lesser-Known Symptoms of menopause

Some of the lesser-known symptoms of menopause can be even more confusing because you don't make the automatic connection between symptom and cause. Often these can't be easily explained but they include the following;
Pins and needles/ Tingling extremities
Itchy skin
Forgetfulness
Dizziness
Aching joints
Breast Pain
Bladder incontinence
Hair thinning
Breaking fingernails

The confusion of complacency

It has taken me over two years to face the reality of the menopause and what it brings. Trying to make sense of it can be difficult. I went through most of the change blissfully unaware, which means I am looking back in retrospect to get any clues as to when it may have happened and how I missed these signs. Behind the well-known signs and symptoms lie a few hidden hurdles that are less talked about. On reading about these I can look back and see that some of these have been very present features in my life. The problem is in your late twenties you don't expect to be going through the menopause, so instead, your overactive brain attaches different meanings to what is happening. Unfortunately, at the time I was going through the menopause, I was also studying to be a doctor, so I was at a very dangerous stage of thinking I knew a lot about some things and in reality, I knew very little about most.

One of the lesser-known symptoms is the sensation of "tingling extremities" and I vividly remember convincing myself that I had the early onset of a neurological condition because I was getting these regular unexplained pins and needles. None of my friends seemed to be getting them, and we had recently studied our neurology module, so my brain was pushed into overdrive. It was scary at the time. You don't feel like you can talk to anyone about it because they would think you were crazy and overreacting. Then you end

Some Science: Bones and Hormones

Oestrogen as a hormone helps to protect against bone loss. As we age, we all lose bone tissue and bones become thinner and weaker (osteoporosis). This leaves you at greater risk of a fracture. Women are already at a disadvantage to men because they lose bone tissue more rapidly, but this risk is amplified following the menopause when oestrogen levels dramatically fall.

Crumbly Bones

Being sent for a DEXA scan at the age of thirty-one was a harsh wake up call. A DEXA scan is a bone density scan which looks to see how strong your bones are. In the politest possible way, this is something we send our elderly patients for as they approach the later stages of life. Turning thirty you are already mourning the loss of your youthful twenties, so to then be given an appointment for a DEXA scan is taken like a slap in the face. You've been convincing yourself for the best part of a year you aren't getting old, you're entering your prime decade of life, ready to shine and take on the world, and then you get told your bones may be crumbling beneath you.

The reason you need to assess your bone strength is because women going through the menopause have reduced levels of oestrogen which increases the risk of osteoporosis and subsequently increases your risk of fracture. These aren't issues I ever imagine having to contend with at the age of thirty. My life is busy, I have enough to worry about between work, exams, socialising and my desperate attempts to remain a balanced human being. There is already enough pressure to work out in order to stay skinny and keep healthy. It is already a struggle to find time in a day when you start work at seven thirty and leave twelve to thirteen hours later after being on your feet all day. It's a struggle to choose to go to the gym after work rather than to catch up with friends over a glass of wine. Living in London is expensive and paying for a gym can really sting. It's OK in the summer, but during the winter when your only day light hours are spent at work inside a hospital, what choice do you have. We all know we need to find that time to exercise regularly to avoid gaining weight and living an unhealthy life, but now thanks to those declining oestrogen levels there is an additional guilt to contend with...

If you don't find the time to exercise regularly, your bones may crumble before you've successfully completed your third decade of life.

So, I won't be going for that glass of wine after work then.

There are ways to minimise the risks of osteoporosis, as well as the above-mentioned exercise, starting on regular HRT can reduce the risk and well as calcium and vitamin D supplements to keep your body in balance.

Some Science: Vagina

Following menopause there are significant changes to a women's genital area. The fall in oestrogen causes the vaginal tissues to become thinner and drier, something referred to as atrophic vaginitis. This can lead to symptoms of dryness and itchiness down below, painful intercourse, more frequent urination and even recurrent urinary infections.

The intimacies of menopause

One symptom that I definitely experienced early on was vaginal dryness. This is something around 50% of women experience during and after menopause, but it is not something you envisage experiencing as a young woman. For me this started in my late twenties, and I was mortified. I was mortified because at the time I was in a relationship, and couldn't understand why it was happening. I wasn't unhappy in my relationship, but physical issues like this can cause a lot of trust and emotional upset between you and your partner, especially when it occurs at such a young age completely out of the blue. I felt so guilty at the time and had no understanding why this was happening. I couldn't talk to anyone about it, I was young; this shouldn't be happening to me. The dryness had also made sex painful, and I assumed I must be having regular attacks of thrush. In hindsight I probably over treated myself on numerous occasions for something that wasn't even ever there. I was so ashamed. I also couldn't understand why I was getting these repeated bouts of thrush. I didn't seek medical help because of this shame, but even if I had found the courage to go to my GP, would they have thought "ahh a bout of early menopause". It's unlikely that when presented with a woman in her late twenties, who has a dry vagina, the first condition you would jump to is POI. Common things are common. I'm not sure anyone would have correctly identified the root cause of my vaginal dryness at this given point in time. This is again why it is so important to raise awareness of the signs and symptoms that may present for those going through it and for the health professionals who have a responsibility to treat them.

Unsurprisingly the thrush treatment didn't work. I had to start using lube in an attempt to relive the discomfort, but this was done with lacings of judgement, hurt and disdain. The emotional pressures that such a physical thing can have in a relationship should not be underestimated. There's a loss of trust in each other, are you not attracted to one another any more, have your feelings changed? At the time there's no way of knowing this is all down to a chemical process wreaking havoc in your body. I had no clue that this was related to the menopause until years later when I finally got a diagnosis. Years of self-doubt and insecurities within relationships all misunderstood and miscommunicated.

As soon as the connection was made, it was simple, I was prescribed vaginal oestrogen pessaries, and the problem went away. Such a simple intervention ending years of anxiety. When you go through something at an unexpected time, you are constantly beating yourself up about the symptoms because you don't understand them. It really promotes an unhealthy hate relationship with your body, because when you don't understand your body it is easy to turn on her.

The other issues associated with menopause are loss of libido. At the time I was going through a menopause, I was also at the later stages of a long-term relationship. It is a confusing time, you don't know what feelings and emotions to attach to what. You can only look back in hindsight and make assumptions about root causes for certain things, there's no way of knowing if x necessarily caused y, however, if I'd had more of awareness about what my body was going through physically at the time, I think I would have placed less of a burden on myself emotionally.

I am Broken

My biggest struggle over the last few years hasn't been trying to contend with the fact I can't have children. It's been the feeling that I am broken, my body is broken. This was my biggest fear in sharing the diagnosis with anyone. I remember when I was put in touch with the fertility counsellor, she was so kind and caring, but I just felt like everyone was missing the point. Everyone was concerned because I must feel terrible that I couldn't have children, but this wasn't my main concern. I was not at a point where I was thinking about having children. My main worry was that people would think my insides were broken. I wasn't the complete package any more, there was a bit of me missing, something I couldn't offer and there was nothing I could do to fix it. I couldn't work harder, study harder, push myself harder physically to achieve this goal. It was done, this part of me was gone.

I remember in my first counselling session with the fertility specialist, she was sharing all the ways I could still go onto to have children, egg donation, adoption, etc, but I just felt like no one was listening, no one understood why I was upset. It wasn't directly the fact I couldn't have children the traditional way, I was mourning the fact my body was now broken, part of me was redundant, and there was nothing in my control to fix it.

Reconnecting with your body

I've talked about the many ways in which going through the menopause can force you to disconnect with your body, so how are you supposed to rebuild that relationship and reconnect with yourself?

I have found the most grounding way to do this is through yoga and mindfulness. I have dipped in and out of yoga for years, I always enjoyed it but never set aside the time for regular sessions. This changed during lockdown, when we all found we had a lot more time and a lot less options available for what we could do. Lockdown gave everyone a pause on life. We were forced to stop charging blindly through our hectic schedules, to stop and to reflect on what was important. At this time, I was also juggling a busy COVID rota working in a hospital, so I was finding things stressful to say the least. In an attempt to ground myself amongst all this change, I started to do yoga on a regular basis. I found a channel on YouTube which worked well for me, and I found that almost instantly my stress levels decreased. I continued with this for about a year and I really found a positive change in my general mental health and wellbeing.

Now during this time in my life, I was still trying to ignore the fact I had POI. Yes, I was taking my daily HRT, but I had reasoned that in my brain because it was just a continuation of the COCP which I had taken for years. Emotionally I still hadn't decided to face up to the changes my body was going through.

As lockdown eased and life returned to a more normal pace, I dropped off with the yoga sessions and would manage only the odd hot yoga on an occasional Saturday morning. Because life was full pelt again, it was easy to get back into bad habits and push problems below the surface rather than facing them up front. The thing with running away from your problems is that ultimately, they will always catch up with you. Alas, despite the busy workings of everyday life, the underlying anxiety and discontent began to resurface. I had to press pause again. I had to reflect on how I had managed this in the past and what worked for me. I started doing regular yoga sessions, again, and took ten minutes at the end of each day to listen to a mindfulness app before bed. Low and behold my mood improved, my sleep pattern regulated, and I found myself in a more positive mindset.

I think it is the process of active decision making to take that time out of your day and to focus on something completely removed from your daily routine that allows you to time to settle. Yoga allows me time in my day to connect with my body, appreciate and respect my body and care for my body. It is the perfect way to heal any disconnect or rifts that may have built up through the day. Mindfulness allows me to disconnect my brain from body and to just be present in the moment, the calmness and content you can feel at this point I have not been able to reach any other way. Being one with your body is about showing self-love and self-care to yourself. However, you are able to do this it is important to find time in the day to solidify this bond because you and your body have to be in harmony working together to overcome whatever life throws.

A "Pause" on dating

Dating in your thirties is a difficult chapter. The pool of eligible men and women seems to be getting smaller and smaller by the day. To compound this, the older you get, the more bullshit you can see through and the less tolerant you become towards those who are trying to waste your precious time.

Then throw "an inability to conceive children" into the mix and the stakes get even higher.

It's ironic. Many young men don't appear to want children, yet taking that option off the table completely becomes an issue. I remember a conversation with some good friends, they were nice guys, great guys in fact, I have a lot of time for them. We were sat chatting about dating apps and their automatic default was to swipe left for anyone around the age of thirty-three to thirty-five "because they'd obviously be wanting children" (swiping left means an automatic reject). I couldn't believe what I was hearing. They were just cutting women from their pool based on age alone because they'd made a sweeping assumption, they knew what that women of a certain age wanted. They hadn't even said hello, engaged in any form of conversation, just assumed and swiped. As a thirty-four-year-old who was currently active on the dating apps, my heart sank, if two "decent" men were sitting here saying this, what hope in hell did we women have of finding anyone.

It also made me angry based on the obvious ignorant assumptions being cast; they hadn't even stopped to consider does she even want children? Or god forbid can she even have them? They were making an overriding generalisation about what they thought women wanted and applying it to every woman they came into contact with. This didn't strike me as a hurdle in the dating game, a hurdle is something you can jump over, this is more like a deep pothole in the road to love, one that once you've been pushed down you can't get out of. You're thirty-four, oh well into the pot hole you go, no more questions asked.

The limits of fertility on dating appear to be unconsciously present from the offset. But even if by some miracle you do manage to find someone to make those initial steps with the fear of what is to follow is overpowering. If you are in a relationship with someone and you are trying for children and you both discover you are unable to conceive, then you make that journey with someone that already loves you. They have fallen in love with you already, you've already shared your dreams for a future, whatever that may look like be it with or without children. If you then find out together years down the line that you can't bear a child, you can explore the options together supporting one another each step of the way. I'm not trying to say that's an easy journey for anyone and the heartbreak that this diagnosis can bring is very real for any women single or in a relationship. But as a single woman in your thirties, how do you market yourself to someone who doesn't already love you when you can't share the same dreams of having that traditional family unit. Surely they'd just go for someone else, they've not fallen in love with you yet, why would they waste their time. They can find someone else with similar traits but who can then give them a child.

If I say any one this to my friends and family, they tell me I'm being an idiot, of course I'll find someone, and the right person "will understand". But they aren't the ones facing this daunting process of separating the wheat from the chaff. It's easy to brush over someone's fears when you will never quite realise or experience them yourself. It's already hard enough to find "the right one", lord know we, women, don't need any more obstacles in the way.

Then what happens when you do find that great guy (or girl), that one in a million. When is the right time to bring all of this up? First date? So all the cards are on the table? I mean why stop there should you have it on your dating profile so everyone's in the know from the outset (although I don't think they've yet created a box for "would like but can't necessarily have children.") But on a serious note, when is the right time to share this. I do worry if you leave it too long, will someone think you've deceived them; think you've been lying to them, is this going to cause future trust issues with someone I've not even met yet? I know I am under no obligation to share anything so private until I am good and ready, but these are issues you have to contend with in your head. Dating doesn't seem so carefree and easy any more. It's lost the innocence, because it's almost like you are harbouring this deep and dark secret from the outset.

Defining your identity

I was recently listening to a podcast about the joys and pressures of being single. It talked about how in recent years there has been a huge increase in the number of single, unmarried women between the ages of twenty-five and fifty-five. It, then, discussed the pressures and stigma socially attached to the notion of single women as they get older. Nothing I hadn't heard before, but it was refreshing to hear a variety of strong independent women, all telling their own stories and sharing their own experiences. The reason I mention it here is because of a comment made by one of the women towards the end of her interview. This one comment made me instantly reframe the way I look at being a single woman in my thirties with no children.

She talked about how through being single it meant she had found more time to spend with her parents and invest in her relationship with them. She had not had to adopt the identity of being a wife or a mother and along with it take on all the additional responsibilities that those roles could bring. She found herself therefore in an interesting paradox. At this later stage in her life when "traditionally" one would have long flown the nest and be consumed by work, kids and marriage she suddenly had a lot more time and energy to invest and spend with her mum and dad.

This got me thinking about my own identify. Rather than mourning the fact I don't have a partner or don't have a child, I should reframe that thinking to celebrate all those things I do still have and all those relationships that are already in my life.

I am, and have been for thirty-four years, a daughter. I can now give 100% of my energy into being the best daughter I can and make the most of that time with my parents. I've gone through times in the past where I have been more distant, be that because I was consumed in a relationship or because work or studying had engrossed me. So why not take this time now when I don't have those distractions to focus on being the best daughter and cherishing every moment I can with them. This doesn't even have to include a physical presence; I live far from both of my parents, but even finding the time to make a brief phone call just to check in is invaluable. Rather than pining after this illustrious romantic partnership and focusing on the things I may be missing because I'm not in one, why not embrace the two people already in my life who show me unconditional love every day and have done since the day I was born. As you grow up, your relationships change along with you. You are no longer the sulky, angry and confused teenager that used to push boundaries with your parents. I've had many years to reflect on what my parents gave up for me as I was growing up and how much of their lives were spent with me as the sole focus. I have a different type of relationship with them now, so why not take advantage of this golden and often missed opportunity to explore and enjoy this new connection.

Another identity I want to celebrate is that I am a friend. I am an only child and from a young age I have always held my friendships very dear. My friends have been the closest thing I have to siblings as I've grown up, and therefore, the bond I have with many of them to this day is unbreakable. Even when I've been in romantic relationships in the past, my friends were still a high priority and I wouldn't have this any other way. So yes, I am single and childless at this present time in my life, but rather than that being a negative notion, I can reframe my thinking. It is time to celebrate the fact that right now I have more time and energy to invest in these friendships. I can nurture close relationships with my friends that would maybe have slipped away if my life had taken a different path such as motherhood or as a wife.

I'm not in any way trying disregard or take away the joys one can get from being a mum or from being in a content romantic relationship, but rather than pinning all your hopes on these two things wouldn't it be refreshing to simply reframe your mindset and place value on those relationships you already have and focus on nurturing the bonds already in place. Every relationship in your life is a gift and it's up to you to recognise the value these already established relationships can bring to your own life.

Hiding away

There is stigma and taboo attached to POI and going through an early menopause. I personally hid from my diagnosis for a number of years, and I hid it from others. I didn't want people to know. They'd surely think I was broken just as I did. How would any guy ever look at me again if he knew my ovaries were all dried up. It took me time to process this myself before I was able to process it with anyone else.

Opening up about my diagnosis is an ongoing struggle for me. To this day I have told close friends and even sometimes others in unexpected circumstances, but it's still not something I've "gone public" with until now. Why is there such a taboo attached to this? We live in an age where it's OK not to want children, not to have children and to have them by different means, be that egg donation or adoption. But there's still something inside that stops you, makes you feel different and makes you not want to share these things so freely. In a society that is supposedly so forward thinking, we are still so regressive in our attitudes towards what makes a successful life. Having a family comes high in societies ideals of making it. Maybe that's what adds to this sense you are broken; you can't do the one thing society is expecting you too. How do you tell society that without judgement and disregard? No one wants to be pitied, but unfortunately, it seems society can't help but pity a woman in her thirties who can't bear child, the one thing she was destined to do. In a world where women are succeeding in life and have a stronger hold in society more than ever, why would any women want to allow society to then pity her.

Maybe I am being overly harsh. Maybe what I perceive as pity is in fact an attempt to empathise with a situation. It is a confusing time that I am still struggling to navigate, and this can cause my views on things to get distorted sometimes. I also at this point want to reiterate how lucky I have been in getting support from my family and friends, they have shown nothing but kindness and compassion and understanding throughout my journey, and for that, I am eternally grateful.

People hide when they are scared, and people are scared of what they don't understand or know. That is why I want to raise more awareness around the issues of POI and early menopause in young women. People need to be aware that this can happen, be aware of what to look out for and be more aware of how they behave towards women who may be going though these things. We need more awareness and more tolerance towards issues that are a very real part of life for so many young women and girls out there. We need to feel supported by friends, family and society so that we don't feel the need to hide away and suffer alone, so that we can live this journey out in the real world free from shame or fear.

Support networks

Whenever you go through a major life event, you turn to your support networks. For me this is largely my friends and family. I am a very open person and I like to talk things through. The problem arises when you can't lean on those support networks the way you have been used too. As human beings when we are supporting each other we often draw on our own life experiences to show that we understand and can empathise. None of my friends (to my knowledge) have been through the experience of an early menopause, so it is very hard for them to directly relate to this. Equally even family members who have been through a menopause won't have been through it at quite the same stage in their life which massively effects the experience had. My friends and family have been brilliant over the last few years and have been available to talk whenever, but it is a difficult conversation to bring up with someone who won't fully understand where you are coming from. I think in part this is why I buried my head in the sand for so long. I didn't think anyone fully understood what I was going through, even my therapist seemed to be attaching meaning to parts of the journey that weren't important to me at that time.

Most of the menopause literature online was directed towards women in a later stage of life, I couldn't relate to these women and I couldn't relate to the issues they were having despite the fact we were going through the same biological process.

This was one of my motivations for starting my blog and for wanting to write this book. To be a voice for those women who can't seem to fit in with anyone else. To be an ear for those women who feel like their journey doesn't match up with the journey of others. To say its OK to feel like you're on your own but you really aren't. There is a charity called 'The Daisy Network' that raise awareness and can offer advice and support for women with POI. There are support networks out there, but these can be hard to find and at a time when your world is turning upside down it can be hard to find the energy to engage, it took me long enough trust me. Just remind yourself there are support networks around, there's no rush, this is your journey, process it in your own time and when you are ready to talk, someone will still be there waiting.

Going it alone

I was single when I discovered by chance that I had POI, and had gone through an early menopause. Ironically, it was following a break up and coming off the COCP that triggered my symptoms and led me to the diagnosis. But regardless of the lead up when I got the diagnosis, I got it as a single women.

This has been my journey. The loss is my own. I wasn't trying for children when I received my diagnosis, I wasn't in a relationship and receiving support from another person as the news was broken. I am not suggesting that it is in any way worse for me than it is for others who may have a partner, but it's definitely a very different journey and the only one I can comment on having gone through it myself.

I could have chosen to have a family member or friend with me when I went to see the specialist, but there was something in me that needed to do this for myself. This was happening to me right now as an independent. I needed to try and cope with this myself, it was my fertility journey and at this point in time it wasn't being shared with anyone else.

It's taken me a few years to face this. I've tried various things. I've tried ignoring it, I've tried therapy, I've tried talking about it with friends and family, but it wasn't until I started writing it all down that it started to make any kind of sense. It wasn't until I reflected back on what I had been through and how various things had made me feel that I was finally able to face this, embrace it and start to move forward in my life.

I understand the pain, I understand the shame you may feel, I understand the detach you experience from your own body and it's OK. It's OK to feel all of these things, but it's also possible to heal them. To heal the pain, remove the shame and reconnect with your body. The early menopause can be a very lonely journey, but it is not one that you have to do alone. Firstly, do it with yourself. Reconnect with your body. Then, do it with your friends and family, open up to them about how you are feeling. And finally, do it with others who are out there. There is a wide network of support available, others who are going through what you are going through, others who have struggled and found a way. You are not alone on this journey and the best is yet to come.

The Future- no longer on pause

Who knows what the future brings for any one of us. The beauty of life is that you never know what's around the corner and anything is possible. We have challenges along the way that we must face, but it is how we overcome these challenges that makes us who we are. I'm not sure what my future brings and what other hurdles I may have to jump to get there, but I know that I am not alone in this journey, and I plan to enjoy every step of the way.